CONTENTS

LAKE CLASSICS

Great American
Short Stories I

Kate
CHOPIN

Stories retold by Emily Hutchinson
Illustrated by Tracy Hall

LAKE EDUCATION
Belmont, California

LAKE CLASSICS

Great American Short Stories I

Washington Irving, Nathaniel Hawthorne, Mark Twain, Bret Harte, Edgar Allan Poe, Kate Chopin, Willa Cather, Sarah Orne Jewett, Sherwood Anderson, Charles W. Chesnutt

Great American Short Stories II

Herman Melville, Stephen Crane, Ambrose Bierce, Jack London, Edith Wharton, Charlotte Perkins Gilman, Frank R. Stockton, Hamlin Garland, O. Henry, Richard Harding Davis

Great British and Irish Short Stories

Arthur Conan Doyle, Saki (H. H. Munro), Rudyard Kipling, Katherine Mansfield, Thomas Hardy, E. M. Forster, Robert Louis Stevenson, H. G. Wells, John Galsworthy, James Joyce

Great Short Stories from Around the World

Guy de Maupassant, Anton Chekhov, Leo Tolstoy, Selma Lagerlöf, Alphonse Daudet, Mori Ogwai, Leopoldo Alas, Rabindranath Tagore, Fyodor Dostoevsky, Honoré de Balzac

Cover and Text Designer: Diann Abbott

Library of Congress Catalog Number: 94-075017
ISBN 1-56103-007-4
Printed in the United States of America
1 9 8 7 6 5 4 3 2 1

Lake Classic Short Stories

"The universe is made of stories, not atoms."

—Muriel Rukeyser

"The story's about you."

—Horace

Everyone loves a good story. It is hard to think of a friendlier introduction to classic literature. For one thing, short stories are *short*—quick to get into and easy to finish. Of all the literary forms, the short story is the least intimidating and the most approachable.

Great literature is an important part of our human heritage. In the belief that this heritage belongs to everyone, *Lake Classic Short Stories* are adapted for today's readers. Lengthy sentences and paragraphs are shortened. Archaic words are replaced. Modern punctuation and spellings are used. Many of the longer stories are abridged. In all the stories, painstaking care has been taken to preserve the author's unique voice.

Lake Classic Short Stories have something for everyone. The hundreds of stories in the collection cover a broad terrain of themes, story types, and styles. Literary merit was a deciding factor in story selection. But no story was included unless it was as enjoyable as it was instructive. And special priority was given to stories that shine light on the human condition.

Each book in the *Lake Classic Short Stories* is devoted to the work of a single author. Little-known stories of merit are included with famous old favorites. Taken as a whole, the collected authors and stories make up a rich and diverse sampler of the story-teller's art.

Lake Classic Short Stories guarantee a great reading experience. Readers who look for common interests, concerns, and experiences are sure to find them. Readers who bring their own gifts of perception and appreciation to the stories will be doubly rewarded.

❦ Kate Chopin ❧
(1851–1904)

About the Author

Kate O'Flaherty was born in St. Louis, Missouri. She was the daughter of an Irish immigrant father and a Creole mother. (The Creoles were descendants of the first French and Spanish colonists in the Gulf States.) After her father died, young Kate was raised in her mother's French-speaking household.

When she was 19, she married Oscar Chopin, a Louisiana cotton trader. They settled first in New Orleans. Later they lived in the nearby bayou country where so many of her stories are set.

For many years, her energies were centered on her family. But when her husband died of swamp fever, she moved back to St. Louis with her six children. Fortunately, her husband had left her enough money to take care of her family. At last, she could begin the literary career that she had been putting off for so long.

In 1889, when she was 38, she published her first story. Often she would finish a story on the same day she started it. She would write longhand on a lapboard. As often as not, she was surrounded by her children. In all, she wrote about 100 short stories that were published in magazines. Many of her stories are about personal acts of rebellion.

Her novel *The Awakening* (1899) brought an end to her writing career, although it is now considered her masterpiece. Its frank portrayal of adultery and mixed marriage created a scandal. The book, in fact, was banned from libraries, and Kate Chopin was shunned by Louisiana society. She wrote very little after that.

If you like reading about characters who seek happiness by taking chances, you'll like Kate Chopin.

The Story of an Hour

Bad news can come as a terrible shock. In this story a woman learns of her husband's death in a train accident. In an instant, she realizes that her whole life will change. How would *you* react to such news? Mrs. Mallard's reaction may surprise you.

THEY TRIED TO BE AS GENTLE AS POSSIBLE IN TELLING
HER THE NEWS OF HER HUSBAND'S DEATH.

The Story of an Hour

Everyone knew that Mrs. Mallard had heart trouble. So they tried to be as gentle as possible in telling her the news of her husband's death.

It was her sister Josephine who told her. Her husband's friend Richards was there, too, standing by. He had been in the newspaper office when news of the train accident was received. Brently Mallard's name was first on the list of the "killed." Richards had hurried at once to Mrs. Mallard's side. He wanted to keep any less careful, less tender friend from telling her the sad news.

She did not deny the news as many women have done. That is, she did not seem to have trouble believing it. She cried at once, suddenly and wildly, in her sister's arms. Then, when the storm of grief was over, she went to her room alone. She would let no one follow her.

She sank into a big comfortable armchair in front of the open window. Suddenly she was so tired that the feeling seemed to reach into her soul.

From the window, she could see the tops of trees. They were full of new spring life. The delicious breath of rain was in the air. From the street below, she could hear someone shouting. The notes of a distant song that someone was singing reached her ears. Countless birds were chirping. Patches of blue sky showed here and there through the clouds.

For a while, she sat with her head thrown back on the pillow of the chair. She was quite still, except when a sob came up into her throat. This would make her shake, the way a child who has cried itself to sleep will keep sobbing in its dreams.

She was a young woman, with a pretty face. As she looked out at the patches of deep blue sky, she started thinking. Something was coming to her, and she was waiting for it. What was it? She did not know. But she felt it, creeping out of the sky. It was reaching to her through the sounds, the smells, and the colors that filled the air.

Slowly she began to get an idea of what it was. It was joy! Over and over, under her breath, she said, "Free, free, free!" Her eyes were bright. Her heart was beating fast, and the blood warmed and relaxed every inch of her body.

She tried to beat back the feeling. She knew that she would cry again when she saw his kind, tender hands folded in death. She would cry when she saw the face that had never looked at her except with love. But she saw past that sad moment to a long parade of years that would belong to her alone. And she opened her arms in welcome to them.

There would be no one to live for her during those coming years. She would live for herself. There would be no strong will bending hers and trying to control her. Now it all seemed so clear. Whether out of kindness or cruelty, no one had the right to control another. She had never thought of that before.

And yet she had felt love for him—sometimes. Often she had not. What did it matter! Love seemed as nothing compared to the new freedom she felt! She now saw this as the strongest feeling she had ever had!

"Free! Body and soul free!" she kept whispering.

Josephine was kneeling before the closed door, asking to come in. "Louise, open the door! I beg you, open the door! You will make yourself ill. What are you doing, Louise? For heaven's sake!"

"Go away. I am not making myself ill." No, she was drinking in life itself through that open window.

She imagined all the days ahead of her. Spring days and summer days and all sorts of days that would be her own. She breathed a quick prayer that life would be long. Only yesterday, she had thought how terrible it would be if life were long.

She stood up, finally, and let her sister in. Without meaning to, she walked as if she were a goddess of Victory. She put her arm around her sister's waist, and they walked down the stairs. Richards stood waiting for them.

Someone was opening the front door with a key. It was Brently Mallard who walked in, carrying his suitcase and umbrella. He was a little worn out from traveling. He had not been near the scene of the accident. He did not even know there had been one. At the sound of Josephine's loud scream, he stood amazed. Richards quickly moved to block his view of his wife.

But Richards was too late.

When the doctors came, they said she had died of heart disease—of joy that kills.

The Recovery

How would it feel to regain
your eyesight after 15 years
of blindness? Surely it
would be wonderful in
every way—or would it?
Perhaps you might have to
look at something you never
wanted to see.

SHE WANTED TO LOOK AT THE THINGS OF NATURE
BEFORE LOOKING INTO THE EYES OF HER LOVED ONES.

The Recovery

She was a woman of 35 who still had some of the beauty of youth. She had, of course, lost that fresh look she once had. But her face had a young expression.

For the past 15 years she had lived in darkness with closed eyelids. Then—by one of those miracles of science—her sight had been given back to her. Now, for the first time in many years, she could see. She opened her eyes upon the full brightness of a June day.

The woman was alone. She had asked to be alone at the very first. She was very happy—but she was also afraid. The first thing she wanted to see was the light from her open window. She wanted to look at the things of nature before looking into the eyes of her loved ones.

And how beautiful was the world from her open window!

"Oh, my God!" she whispered, as she was overcome with happiness. There were no words that could tell her feelings at that moment. When she saw the blue June sky, she felt a joy that was almost holy. Then she looked at the rolling meadows, gold and green, reaching deep into the purple distance. Near her window, the maple leaves rippled in the sun. Flowers, rich and warm in color, grew under her window. Colorful butterflies stopped in mid-air.

"The world has not changed," she thought to herself. "It has only grown more beautiful. Oh, I had forgotten how beautiful!"

All the things she remembered were in her room. Her wooden table, bright and shiny, stood just where it had been

15 years ago. A crystal vase of roses and a few books were on top of it. The sight of chairs, beds, pictures, carpets, and drapes gave her keen joy.

She touched the French clock that stood on the mantel over the fireplace. She looked at the bronze figure of an old-fashioned gentleman posing next to the dial. Now she greeted him as an old friend. As a child she had liked him. At a later age, she thought he was an example of bad art. Now, nothing could have made her part with the old French clock and its little bronze man.

The mirror was over there in the corner. She had not forgotten it, but she was afraid to look into it. For a moment she stayed back, as a young girl on her way to confession is ashamed and afraid. But she had not forgotten.

"This is foolish," she said suddenly. She forced herself to cross the room and looked at her face in the glass.

"Mother!" she cried, turning around quickly. But she was alone. She took a deep breath and wiped her forehead with her handkerchief. With shaking hands, she held onto the back of a low chair. Then she looked into the mirror again.

Anyone looking at the same face in the mirror would have seen an attractive woman of 35 or more. Only God knows what the woman saw. It was something that held her with terrible fascination.

The eyes, above all, seemed to speak to her. They alone seemed to belong to that old, other self that was now gone forever. As she looked into her own eyes, she thought, "They lied. They all lied to me. Mother, sisters, Robert—all, all of them lied."

When the eyes in the mirror had nothing more to tell her, she looked away. The fresh, sweet look in her face had changed. It was not as pretty as it had been before. Her confidence was gone.

The next day, she took a walk with the man who had loved her for years. Before she became blind, she had promised to marry him. But after she lost her sight, she would not keep her promise. Yet he had not wanted any other woman for his wife. So he stayed by her side, just to be close to her.

He was five years older than she, but he was in very good shape. His face had become even better looking with the addition of a few strong lines. White hairs were beginning to show among the black ones on his temples.

They walked across a flat lawn toward a seat in the garden. She had not said much since she had looked at herself in the mirror. Nothing could surprise her after that. Now she was ready to see the changes that the years had brought to all of them—mother, sisters, friends.

He led her to the bench. He had important things to say to her, and he wanted her full attention.

He took her hand in his. She was used to this and did not pull it away, but let it lie there.

"Do you remember our old plans, Jane?" he began. "Do you remember all that we wanted to do and see? We would start our travels in the early spring and come back with the frosts of winter. You have not forgotten, dearest?" He bent his face down over her hand and kissed it. "The spring of our lives is over. But we still have the summer—and, God willing, the fall and the winter ahead of us. Tell me, Jane—tell me—speak to me!" he begged.

"I—oh, Robert," she said. "Wait. The sight of things confuses me. I am not used to it. I must go back into the dark to think."

He still held her hand, but she had turned half away from him. She buried her face in her arm, which she had leaned on the back of the garden seat.

What could she hope to find in the darkness that she did not find in the light? She might hope, she might wait, and she might pray. But hoping and praying and waiting would not help her.

The light had given her back the world, life, and love. But it had also robbed her of her dreams, and it had stolen away her youth.

He held her close, pressing his face near hers for his answer. All that he heard was a little low sob.

The Locket

Have you ever had a truly precious possession? Did that object seem to have special powers to comfort you or keep you safe? In this story, a young woman gives her locket to her sweetheart. Will her keepsake keep him safe as he goes off to war?

"What's that you have around your neck, Ned?
Is it your sweetheart's picture?"

The Locket

I

One night in autumn a few men stood around a fire on the side of a hill. They were part of a small group of Confederate soldiers, waiting for orders to march. Their gray uniforms were old and worn out. One of the men was heating something in a tin cup over the fire. Two men were lying down on the grass, and a fourth was trying to read a letter. He had opened the buttons of his flannel shirt.

"What's that you have around your neck, Ned?" asked one of the men who were lying down.

Ned—or Edmond—closed one of the buttons of his shirt and did not answer. He went on reading his letter.

"Is it your sweetheart's picture?"

"It's no girl's picture," said the man at the fire. He had finished heating his food and was stirring it with a small stick. "It's a charm—some kind of hoodoo business that a priest gave him to keep him out of trouble. I know those Catholics. That's why Frenchy has never been injured. Hey, French! Isn't that right?" Edmond looked up from his letter.

"What is it?" he asked.

"Isn't that a charm you're wearing around your neck?"

"It must be, Nick," said Edmond with a smile. "I don't know how I could have gotten through this year and a half without it."

The letter had made Edmond heartsick and homesick. He lay down on his back and looked up at the stars. But he was not thinking of the stars. He was thinking of a certain spring day when the bees were humming in the flowers. On that lovely day, a girl was saying good-bye to him.

He could see her clearly in his imagination. He remembered how she took the locket from her neck and put it around his neck. It was an old-fashioned golden locket. Inside were pictures of her mother and father. Their names and the date of their marriage were carved inside the locket. The locket was her most precious possession. Edmond could feel again the folds of the girl's white dress.

He could see the droop of the sleeves as she put her fair arms around his neck. Her sweet face, showing the pain of parting, appeared before him as clearly as if she were there. With a deep sigh, he turned over and buried his face in his arms. He lay there still and motionless.

That night, he dreamed that his fair Octavie had brought him a letter. He had no chair to offer her, and he was ashamed of the way he was dressed. He was embarrassed at the poor food he had to offer. He dreamed that a snake was wrapping itself around his throat. When he tried to grab it, the snake slithered away. Then his dream ended.

"Get up, Frenchy!" Nick was screaming in his face. The hill was alive with noise and action. In the east the sun was rising out of the darkness. The light was still dim in the plain below.

"What's it all about?" wondered a big black bird, sitting in the top of the tallest tree. He was one of the old and wise ones. But he was not wise enough to guess what all the noise meant. So all day long, he kept on blinking and wondering.

The terrible noise reached far out over the plain and across the hills. It woke the little babies that were sleeping in their cradles. Dark trails of smoke curled up toward the sun and cast a shadow on the plain. The foolish young birds thought it was going to rain, but the wise one knew better.

As night fell, all the men had vanished, along with the noise and smoke. Then the old bird understood! With a flap of his great, black wings, he flew downward. He circled toward the plain.

A man was picking his way across the field. He was dressed in the dark clothes of a priest. His job was to offer the comfort of religion to any of the men who might still be alive. A raggedly dressed helper was with him. This man was carrying a bucket of water and a jug of wine.

There were no wounded here. They had all been taken away. And the retreat of the soldiers had been very fast. The vultures and the two men would have only the dead to attend to.

There was a soldier—just a boy—lying with his face to the sky. His hands were grabbing the grass on either side of his body. His fingernails were packed with earth and bits of grass. He had no hat, and his face and clothing were dirty. Around his neck hung a gold chain and locket. The priest, bending over the boy, took the chain from the soldier's neck.

He had grown used to the terrors of war. Now he could face them. But the sorrows of war always brought tears to his dim, old eyes.

The church bells were ringing half a mile away. The priest and his helper knelt down on the grass. They said a prayer for the dead as well as their regular evening prayers.

II

The peace and beauty of a spring day had fallen on the earth like a blessing. The sun shone on a tree-lined road near a small stream in Louisiana. There, an old-fashioned carriage pulled by fat black horses rumbled slowly along. Inside the carriage sat the fair Octavie and her old neighbor, Judge Pillier. As Ned's father and her friend, he had come to take her for a morning drive.

Octavie wore a plain black dress with long sleeves. A narrow belt circled her waist. Since she had stopped wearing her hoopskirt, she now looked something like a nun. Under the folds of her dress rested the old locket. She never wore it now. She had come to think of it as a holy thing. What had happened had made it even more precious.

The locket had come back to her with a letter. A hundred times she had read it over. Just that morning she had read it again. As she sat by the carriage window, she had smoothed the letter out on her knee. Closing her eyes, she noticed the smell of spices and other heavy odors in the air. She could hear the songs of birds and the humming of insects.

She was so young and the world was so beautiful. A strange feeling came over her as she read the priest's letter again and again. It didn't seem real.

The priest told of that autumn day drawing to its close. He described the gold and the red colors in the sky. He told her how the night gathered its shadows to cover the faces of the dead. Oh! She still could not believe that one of those dead was her own! To think of her dear Ned, lying there looking up at the gray sky!

Why was the spring here with its flowers, if he was dead! Why was she here? What more did she have to do with life and the living?

Octavie had felt many moments like this, and they always ended the same way.

"I shall grow old and quiet and sad like poor Aunt Tavie," she said to herself. She folded the letter and put it back in the desk.

Then again, Octavie was hit by that terrible feeling of loss she had felt so often before. The soul of her youth clamored for its rights! She wanted her share in the glory and joy of the world. She leaned back and pulled her veil a little closer about her face. It was an old black veil of her Aunt Tavie's.

"Will you do me a favor, Octavie?" asked the judge. "Would you take off that veil? It seems out of place, somehow, with the beauty and promise of the day."

The young girl did as the older man asked. She took the veil from her hat, folded it neatly, and put it on the seat beside her.

"Ah! That is better! Far better!" he said. "Never put it on again, dear." Octavie felt a little hurt. It seemed that he wished to keep her from sharing the suffering of the family.

The carriage had left the big road and turned into a level plain that had once been a meadow. Groups of trees were here and there. They were beautiful in their spring glory. Cattle were grazing in spots where the grass was tall. At the far end of the meadow was a lilac hedge. It lined the road that led to Judge Pillier's house. The scent of its heavy flowers met them like a soft and tender hug of welcome.

As they got close to the house, the old gentleman placed an arm around the girl's shoulders. He turned her face up to him. "On a day like this," he said, "do you not think miracles might happen?

The whole earth is alive with the renewal of spring. On such a day, do you think that heaven, for once, might give us back our dead?" He spoke to her in a low, serious voice. She looked at him with eyes that were full of longing and a certain terror of joy.

The horses started trotting a little faster as they got closer to home. As the carriage turned into the drive, a whole flock of birds started singing.

Octavie felt as if she were floating in a dream—a dream more real than life. Just ahead was the old gray house with its sloping roof. Behind it was a blur of green. She saw familiar faces and heard voices as if they came from far away.

And Edmond was holding her. Her dead Edmond, her living Edmond. She felt the beating of his heart against her and the joy of his tender kisses. She hoped never to awake. It was as if the spirit of life and the springtime had given her back her youth.

Many hours later, Octavie took the locket out of her pocket. She looked at Edmond with a question in her eyes.

"It was the night before a battle," he said. "In the hurry of the fight, and the retreat the next day—I never missed it. When I discovered that it was gone, I thought I had lost it in battle. Later I found out that it had been stolen."

"Stolen," she said. And she thought of the dead soldier looking up at the sky.

Edmond said nothing. But he thought of his fellow soldier, the one far back in the shadow, the one who had said nothing.

A Pair of Silk Stockings

Does spending money on yourself ever make you feel selfish? "Doing for others" is what little Mrs. Sommers does best. She only meant to have a little rest when she sat down in the department store. What made her buy the silk stockings?

IT HAD BEEN A LONG TIME SINCE MRS. SOMMERS HAD
BEEN FITTED WITH GLOVES.

A Pair of Silk Stockings

Little Mrs. Sommers one day found $15 that she didn't know she had. She wasn't expecting to have that much money. It seemed like a lot, and it gave her a feeling of importance. She had not felt so important for years.

The question of how to spend it went around and around in her mind. For a day or two she walked about as if she were in a dream. She did not want to act too quickly—to do anything she might be sorry for later. It was during the still hours of the night that she came up with a good plan for the money.

A dollar or two should be added to the price usually paid for Janie's shoes. The better shoes would last longer than the cheap ones did. Then she would buy yards of fabric to make new clothes for the boys and Janie and Mag. She had been planning just to patch the old clothes—but now things were different.

There would still be enough left for new socks for the children—two pairs each. That would save a lot of mending! She would get caps for the boys and sailor hats for the girls. The thought of her children, looking fresh and new for once in their lives, made her very happy.

Sometimes the neighbors talked about the "better days" that little Mrs. Sommers had known. Of course that was before she even thought of being Mrs. Sommers. She herself never thought of those days. There was no time to think about the past. The needs of the present took up all her energy. Any thought of the future usually scared her—but luckily tomorrow never comes.

Mrs. Sommers was one who knew the value of bargains. She would stand in line for hours to get something that was selling below cost. If need be, she could elbow her way. She had learned to hold on to a piece of goods and stand in line, no matter how long it took.

But that day she was a little faint and tired. Between getting the children fed and getting ready for her shopping spree, she had forgotten to eat lunch.

Now she sat on a chair by a counter in the store. She tried to gather the strength and courage to deal with the crowds of shoppers. A very tired feeling had come over her, and she rested her hand on the counter. She wore no gloves. Slowly she became aware that her hand was resting on something very smooth and pleasant to the touch.

She looked down to see that her hand lay upon a pile of silk stockings. A sign said that their price was reduced from $2.50 to $1.98. A young girl who stood behind the counter asked if she wished to see a pair. Mrs. Sommers smiled. It was just as if she had been asked to see a diamond tiara that she was thinking of buying. She went on feeling the soft, lovely things, with both hands now. She held the stockings up to see them glisten in the light. She felt them glide through her fingers.

Then suddenly her cheeks got red. She looked up at the girl.

"Do you have any in size eight?"

There were many pairs in size eight. In fact, there were more of that size than any other. Here was a light blue pair. There were some lavender, some black, and many shades of tan and gray. Mrs. Sommers looked closely at a black pair.

"A dollar and ninety-eight cents," she said out loud. "Well, I'll take this pair." She handed the girl a five-dollar bill and waited for her change. What a very small package the girl handed to her! It seemed lost when she put it in her shabby old shopping bag.

After that, Mrs. Sommers did not go to the bargain counter. She took the elevator to the upper floor and went into the women's rest room. There, in a corner, she took off her cotton stockings and put on her new silk ones. She was not thinking about why she was doing this. She was not thinking at all. For a time she seemed to be taking a rest from the responsibilities of her life.

How good was the touch of the silk on her skin! She felt like lying back in the chair and enjoying the feel of it. For a little while she did just this. Then she put her shoes back on, rolled the cotton stockings up, and threw them into her bag. Next she went directly to the shoe department. There she took a seat and waited to be fitted.

She was very hard to please. She looked down at the polished boots with pointed toes. Carefully, she held back her long skirts and turned her feet one way and her head another way. Her foot and ankle looked very pretty. She could hardly believe that she was wearing such fine shoes. She wanted a perfect fit and a shoe that was in style, she told the clerk. She said the price didn't matter, as long as she got what she wanted.

It had been a long time since Mrs. Sommers had been fitted with gloves. On those few times that she had bought a pair, they were always "bargains." They were so cheap that it would have been foolish to expect a clerk to fit them to her hand.

Now she rested her elbow on the glove counter. A saleswoman put a kid glove on her hand. She smoothed the fine leather down over the wrist and buttoned it neatly. Both women lost themselves for a second or two as they admired the small gloved hand.

And there were other places where money might be spent.

There were books and magazines piled up in a window a few steps down the street. Now Mrs. Sommers bought two expensive magazines. They were the kind she had read when she was used to other pleasant things. Now she carried them instead of putting them in her bag.

As well as she could, she lifted her skirts at the crossings. The sight of her stockings and boots and well-fitting gloves made her feel good. The fine things gave her a feeling of confidence. She had a sense that she belonged among the well-dressed people.

Mrs. Sommers was very hungry. Any other time, she would have waited until she got home. There, she would have made a cup of tea and had a snack of whatever was around. But the way she was feeling now, that just would not do.

There was a restaurant at the corner. Mrs. Sommers had never been inside it. From the outside, she had seen white linen and shining crystal. Sometimes she had watched the soft-stepping waiters as they served people of fashion.

When she entered the restaurant, no one seemed surprised at her appearance, as she had feared. She seated herself at a small table alone. At once a waiter came to take her order. She did not want much—just a nice, tasty bite. She ordered six blue-point oysters and a lamb chop. Then she told the waiter she wanted something sweet for dessert—perhaps a crème frappé. She also ordered a glass of Rhine wine. Afterwards, she had a small cup of black coffee.

While waiting to be served, Mrs. Sommers took off her gloves very slowly. She laid them carefully on the table. Then she picked up a magazine and looked through it. The restaurant was really very nice. The linen was even whiter than it had seemed through the window. The crystal glasses were even more sparkling.

All around her there were quiet ladies and gentlemen dining at other small tables like hers. No one seemed to notice her. The soft, pleasing sound of music could be heard. A gentle breeze was blowing through the window. She tasted a bit of the delicious food, and she read a word or two. She sipped the wine and wiggled her toes in the silk stockings.

Today the price made no difference. She counted out the money for the waiter and left a tip on his tray. He bowed before her as if she were a princess of royal blood.

There was still some money in her purse. When she saw a poster for an afternoon play, she decided to go.

As she entered the theater, she saw that the play had already begun. An usher led her to a seat. She sat with beautifully dressed women who had gone there to kill time, eat candy, and show off their clothes. Many others were there just to enjoy the play and the acting. It is safe to say that no one enjoyed the play as much as Mrs. Sommers did.

She enjoyed everything—the stage, the actors, and the people in the audience. She laughed at the jokes and cried at the sad parts. She talked a bit to the woman next to her, who offered little Mrs. Sommers some of her candy.

The play was over, the music stopped, and the people left the theater. It was as if a dream had ended. People went off in all directions. Mrs. Sommers went to the corner and waited for the cable car.

A man sat across from her on the cable car. He seemed to be studying her small, pale face. In truth, he saw nothing—unless he was clever enough to see what she was wishing. Her wish was that the cable car would never stop anywhere, but go on and on with her forever.

A Matter of Prejudice

Sometimes adults put up walls that can only be torn down by children. This story is about a stubborn old woman with many strong opinions. Then a sick little girl comes into her life. What lesson does the old woman learn about the price of prejudice?

OLD MADAME CARAMBEAU WAS A WOMAN OF MANY PREJUDICES. SHE HAD SO MANY IT WOULD BE HARD TO NAME THEM ALL.

A Matter of Prejudice

Madame Carambeau did not want to be disturbed by Gustave's birthday party. They carried her big rocking chair to the front of the house. That way, she could look out at the Mississippi River instead of at the backyard. The children would be playing in the backyard.

The house was an old Spanish one in the French Quarter of New Orleans. It was wide, low, and surrounded by a big porch. The land around the house was covered with plants and flowers. A big fence with iron spikes on top kept anyone from looking in.

Madame Carambeau's daughter, Madame Cécile Lalonde, was a widow. Since her husband had died, she had lived with her mother. Every year, Madame Lalonde gave her little son, Gustave, a birthday party. It was the one thing she did that her mother didn't like.

Old Madame Carambeau was a woman of many prejudices. She had so many that it would be hard to name them all. She didn't like dogs, cats, organ grinders, white servants, or children's noises. She hated Americans, Germans, and all people of faiths different from her own. Anything that wasn't French had no right to exist, she thought.

She had not spoken to her son Henri for 10 years. That was because he had married an American girl from Prytania Street. No green tea was ever served in Madame Carambeau's house. Anyone who could not—or would not—drink coffee might drink rosewater for all she cared.

Even so, the children seemed to be having it all their own way that day. The organ grinders were playing in the back yard. Old madame, in her corner, could hear the screams and the laughing. The sound of music was more than she liked. She rocked herself back and forth and hummed a song.

The old madame was straight and slender. Her hair was white, and she wore it in little puffs. Her skin was fair, and her eyes were blue and cold.

Suddenly, she heard footsteps coming toward her. There were not only footsteps, but screams! Then two little children, one chasing after the other, ran up to her.

The first child, a pretty little girl, jumped into Madame Carambeau's lap. She threw her arms around the old lady's neck. The other child then ran up. She tapped her friend with a "last tag" and ran away, laughing.

The most natural thing would have been for the child to get off madame's lap. Any other child would have run after her friend. But this little girl did not do so. She stayed there, panting and fluttering, like a frightened bird.

Madame was greatly annoyed. She moved as if to put the child down. She scolded the child for being rude. The little one did not understand French, so she was not upset. She stayed on in madame's lap. She put her plump little cheek against the soft white linen of the old lady's dress.

Her cheek was very hot and very red. It was dry, too, and so were her hands. The child's breathing was quick and irregular. Madame noticed these signs of illness right away.

Although she might have been a person of prejudice, the old madame was a good nurse. She knew a lot about health, and she was proud of this talent. Even an organ grinder would have been treated with tender care if he had told her he was sick.

Madame's manner toward the little one changed right away. Her arms and her lap were at once extended to become a comfortable resting place. Rocking very gently, she fanned the child with her palm leaf fan. She sang a little song.

The child was quite happy to lie still and talk in that language that madame didn't like. But the brown eyes were soon very sleepy. The little body grew heavy as the child slept in madame's arms.

Madame Carambeau carried the sleeping girl to her own room. The room was large, airy, and inviting. With the child still in her arms, Madame pulled a bell-cord. Then she stood waiting, swaying back and forth. Soon an old servant answered the call. She wore gold hoops in her ears and a bright bandanna wrapped around her head.

"Louise, turn down the bed," said madame. "Place that small, soft pillow near the head. Here is a poor sick child. I think that heaven must have driven her into my arms." She carefully put the child down on the bed.

"Ah, those Americans! Do they deserve to have children? They do not even understand how to take care of them!" said madame. "There, you see, Louise, she is burning up! Open up her buttons while I lift her.

"Ah, talk to me of such parents! So stupid they did not see a fever like that coming on! Instead, they dress their child up like a monkey. Then they send her to play and dance to the music of organ grinders.

"Be careful how you take off her shoes, Louise! Be gentle. Now go to Madame Lalonde and tell her to send me one of Gustave's soft nightgowns."

When Louise left, madame kept busy. She made some juice for the child and got some water ready to sponge her.

Madame Lalonde herself came with the nightgown. She was a pretty, blonde, plump little woman. She didn't seem to have much of a will of her own. But she was mildly distressed at what her mother had done.

"But, mamma! The child's parents will be sending the carriage for her soon. Really, there was no reason for this. Oh, dear! Oh, dear!"

If the bedpost had spoken to Madame Carambeau, she would have paid more attention. Madame Lalonde had never been able to make her mother listen to her.

"Yes, the little one will be quite comfortable in this," said the old lady. She took the nightgown from her daughter.

"But, mamma! What shall I say? What shall I do when they come for her? Oh, dear. Oh, dear!"

"Say what you like," said madame. "I am only thinking of a sick child. As you see, she happens to be under my roof! I think I know my duty at this time of life, Cécile."

As Madame Lalonde had said, the carriage came quickly. An English coachman was driving it, and a red-cheeked Irish maid sat inside. Madame would not even let the maid see the little girl. She had an idea—all her own—that the Irish voice is distressing to the sick.

Madame Lalonde sent the maid away with a long letter to the parents. The letter must have been a good one, for the child was left in Madame Carambeau's care. The child was sweet, gentle and loving. She did cry a little for her mother during the night. But she seemed to take kindly to madame's care. It was not much of a fever. After two days, the child was well enough to go back to her home.

Madame had taken care of many sick people. But she had never before nursed one of those American children she so despised. The trouble was that—after the child left—madame could think of nothing about her to despise. There was, of course, the fact that she was American. But that couldn't be helped. There was also the fact that she didn't speak French. But that wasn't really her fault, either.

Madame thought of the touch of her soft baby arms and the sound of her voice. She remembered how the child kissed her, thinking she was with her mother. These thoughts broke the crust of madame's prejudice and reached her heart.

Often she walked around her house, looking out across the wide river. Sometimes she strolled through her garden that was almost like a tropical jungle. At such moments, the seed began to work in her soul. It was a seed planted by the innocent hands of a little child.

The first shoot that the seed sent forth was Doubt. Madame plucked it away once or twice. But then it would grow again. Then, finally, came the flower of Truth. It was a very beautiful flower. It bloomed on Christmas morning.

Madame Carambeau and her daughter were about to ride to church in their carriage. The old lady gave an order to her coachman, François. Every Sunday morning for many years he had driven these ladies to the French cathedral. He had forgotten exactly how many years. But it had been since Madame Lalonde was a little girl. His surprise was great when Madame Carambeau said to him, "François, today you will drive us to one of the American churches."

"Excuse me, madame?" said the coachman. He thought something was wrong with his hearing.

"I said, you will drive us to one of the American churches. Any one of them," she added, with a wave of her hand. "I suppose they are all alike."

Madame Lalonde was as surprised as the coachman. But she didn't say anything.

François drove them to St. Patrick's Church on Camp Street. As they entered the building, Madame Lalonde looked and felt like a fish out of water. Madame Carambeau, on the other hand, looked as if she had been going to St. Patrick's Church all her life. She sat calmly through the long service and the long sermon. She understood not a word that was spoken.

When the mass was ended, she and her daughter walked toward their carriage.

Then Madame Carambeau turned and spoke to the coachman.

"François, you will now drive us to the home of my son, Henri. No doubt Madame Lalonde can tell you where it can be found."

Yes, her daughter Cécile did know— and so did François, for that matter. They drove a very long way out St. Charles Avenue. It was like a strange city to old madame. She had not been in the American quarter for many years.

The morning was a delicious one, soft and mild. The blooming roses were not hidden behind fences that had spikes. But madame did not seem to notice the roses. And she did not seem to notice the beautiful homes that lined the avenue. She held a bottle of smelling salts to her nose. She acted as if she were in the worst, instead of the most beautiful, part of New Orleans.

Henri's house was very modern. It stood away from the street. A well-kept lawn, lined with rare and beautiful plants, was all around it. The ladies got out of the carriage, rang the bell, and waited for the iron gate to be opened.

A white servant let them in. Madame did not seem to mind. She handed the woman a calling card and followed her daughter into the house.

Not once did she show a sign of weakness. Her son, Henri, came at once and took the old lady in his arms. He sobbed and wept upon her neck as only a warm-hearted Creole could. Henri was a big, good-looking man with an honest face. He had warm brown eyes like his dead father's and a strong mouth like his mother's.

Young Mrs. Carambeau came, too. Her sweet, fresh face was full of happiness. She led her little daughter by the hand. It was the "American child" whom madame had nursed so tenderly a month before! Madame had never suspected that the child was other than a stranger to her.

"What a lucky chance that fever was! What a happy accident!" said Madame Lalonde.

"Cécile, it was no accident, I tell you. It was God's will!" said the old madame. No one argued with her.

They all drove back together to eat Christmas dinner in the old family house. Madame held her sweet little granddaughter in her lap. Her son Henri sat facing her, and beside her was her daughter-in-law.

Henri leaned back in the carriage and could not speak. The truth was that he was so full of joy that he could not say a word. He was going back again to the home where he had been born! He had not been there for 10 long years.

Once again, he would hear the water beat against the green river bank. That sound was not like any other that he had ever heard. He remembered sitting in the sweet shadow of the deep, over-hanging roof. He remembered walking through the beauty of the old garden, where he had played as a child. He could hear his mother's voice, calling to him. Now it would be like it was before that day when he had had to choose between mother and wife. No, he could not trust himself to speak.

But his wife talked a lot. Her French was not very good, and it must have been hard for madame to listen to it.

"I am so sorry, Mother," she said, "that our little one does not speak French. It is not my fault, I assure you." She got a little red and then went on. "It—it was Henri who would not let us speak French."

"That is nothing," said madame, pulling the child close to her. "Her grandmother will teach her French. And the child will teach her grandmother English.

"You see, I have no prejudices. I am not like my son. Henri was always a stubborn boy. Heaven only knows how he got to be that way!"

The Kiss

An old saying tells us that we "can't have our cake and eat it, too." In this story, a beautiful young woman wants to have it both ways. She's perfectly willing to marry for money instead of love. But then a passionate kiss almost ruins her plan.

Even though she really didn't like him very much, she knew he was rich. She liked the things that money could buy.

The Kiss

It was still quite light out of doors. But inside, with the curtains closed and the fire burning low, the room was full of deep shadows.

Brantain sat in one of those shadows. The darkness gave him enough courage to keep his eyes on the girl who sat in the firelight.

She was very good-looking, with that fine, rich coloring that true brunettes have. She petted the cat that lay curled up in her lap. She was quite comfortable. From time to time, she looked into the shadow where Brantain sat. They were talking about things that didn't really matter to them. She knew that he loved her. He was the type who wouldn't even think of hiding his feelings.

For the past two weeks he had wanted to be with her all the time. Now she was waiting for him to declare his love—and she was planning to accept him. Even though she didn't really like him very much, she knew he was really rich. She liked the things that money could buy.

During one of the pauses in their talk, the door opened and another young man came in. Brantain knew him quite well. The girl turned her face toward him. A step or two brought him to her side, and he bent over her chair. She didn't realize that he had not seen Brantain in the shadows. Before she could stop him, he gave her a loving, long kiss on the lips.

"I believe," said Brantain, "that I have stayed too long. I—I had no idea—that is, I must say good-bye." He left before she could say a word.

"I didn't see him sitting there, Nattie!" said the young man who had kissed her. "I know this must have been embarrassing for you. But I hope you'll forgive me this once. Why, what's the matter?"

"Don't touch me. Don't come near me," she said in anger. "What do you mean by coming into the house without ringing the bell?"

"I came in with your brother, as I often do," he answered. "We came in the side door. He went upstairs, and I came in here. I was hoping to find you. Do say that you forgive me, Nathalie!"

"Forgive you! You don't know what you are talking about. Let me pass. Whether I ever forgive you depends—it just depends!"

The next time she saw Brantain, it was at a party. She walked straight up to him and said, "Will you let me speak to you a moment or two, Mr. Brantain?" He seemed very unhappy. But then she took his arm and led him away toward a quiet corner. This gave him a ray of hope.

"Maybe I should not have asked to speak to you, Mr. Brantain. But, oh! I have been very unhappy since our last meeting. When I thought of how it must have looked to you, I felt terrible." By now, hope was plainly showing on Brantain's round face.

"Of course, I know it is nothing to you. But for my sake, please understand something. Mr. Harvy is a good friend of the family. He has been for many years. Why, we have always been like cousins— like brother and sister, you might say. He is my brother's best friend. I am sure he thinks that he is part of the family. Oh, I know it is silly to tell you all this," she said, almost crying. "But it makes so much difference to me what you think of—of me."

Her voice had become very low and quite upset. The misery had all but disappeared from Brantain's face.

"Then you really *do* care what I think, Miss Nathalie? May I call you Miss Nathalie?" Brantain asked sweetly. They turned into a long hallway that was lined with tall plants. They walked slowly to the very end of it. When they turned to walk back, Brantain's face was glowing with happiness. Hers looked as if she had just won something.

* * *

Harvy was among the guests at the wedding. He came up to her in a rare moment when she stood alone.

"Your husband has sent me over to kiss you," he said, smiling.

A quick blush came over her face and throat. Harvy went on, "I guess it's natural for a man to be generous on a day such as this. He tells me he doesn't want this marriage to change our friendship. I don't know what you told him—but he has sent me over here to kiss you."

She felt like a chess player who has played a good game and now sees everything turning out as planned. Her eyes were bright and tender as she looked into his face. Her lips looked hungry for the kiss that she was inviting.

"But, you know," Harvy continued. "I didn't say this to Brantain because it would have seemed ungrateful. But I can tell you. I've stopped kissing women. It's dangerous."

Well, she still had Brantain and his money. A person can't have everything in this world. It was a little unreasonable of her to expect it.

Thinking About
the Stories

The Story of an Hour

1. Who is the main character in this story? Who are one or two of the minor characters? Describe each of these characters in one or two sentences.

2. Some stories are packed with action. In other stories, the key events take place in the minds of the characters. Is this story told more through the characters' thoughts and feelings? Or is it told more through their outward actions?

3. Good writing always has an effect on the reader. How did you feel when you finished reading this story? Were you surprised, horrified, amused, sad, touched, or inspired? What elements in the story made you feel that way?

The Recovery

1. What period of time is covered in this story—an hour, a week, several years? What role, if any, does time play in the story?

2. Did the story plot change direction at any point? Explain the turning point of the story.

3. Suppose this story had a completely different outcome. Can you think of another effective ending for this story?

The Locket

1. Compare and contrast at least two characters in this story. In what ways are they alike? In what ways are they different?

2. How important is the background of the story? Is weather a factor in the story? Is there a war going on or some other unusual circumstance? What influence does the background have on the characters' lives?

3. All stories fit into one or more categories. Is this story serious or funny? Would you call it an adventure, a love story, or a mystery? Is it a character study? Or is it simply a picture the author has painted of a certain time and place? Explain your thinking.

A Pair of Silk Stockings

1. The plot is the series of events that takes place in a story. Usually, story events are linked in some way. Can you name an event in this story that was the cause of a later event?

2. What is the title of this story? Can you think of another good title?

3. Suppose that this story was the first chapter in a book of many chapters. What would happen next?

A Matter of Prejudice

1. Interesting story plots often have unexpected twists and turns. What surprises did you find in this story?

2. Many stories are meant to teach a lesson of some kind. Is the author trying to make a point in this story? What is it?

3. Imagine that you have been asked to write a short review of this story. In one or two sentences, tell what the story is about and why someone would enjoy reading it.

The Kiss

1. All stories fit into one or more categories. Is this story serious or funny? Would you call it an adventure, a love story, or a mystery? Is it a character study? Or is it simply a picture the author has painted of a certain time and place? Explain your thinking.

2. Which character in this story do you most admire? Why? Which character do you like the least?

3. An author builds the plot around the conflict in a story. In this story, what forces or characters are struggling against each other? How is the conflict finally resolved?